GW01417547

# WALKING
# BACKWARDS

## POEMS BY
## KEN MCCULLOUGH

*for Alec*

*" I love these days of white space,*
*empty pages waiting...."*

*with affection,*

*Ken*

*26:X:06*

BLUE LIGHT PRESS ◆ 1ST WORLD LIBRARY

1ˢᵗ WORLD
LIBRARY
Literary Society

AUSTIN ◆ FAIRFIELD ◆ DELHI

WINNER OF THE 2004 BLUE LIGHT BOOK AWARD

# WALKING BACKWARDS

Copyright ©2005 By Ken McCullough

1ST WORLD LIBRARY
PO Box 2211, Fairfield, Iowa 52556
www.1stworldlibrary.com

BLUE LIGHT PRESS
PO Box 642, Fairfield, Iowa 52556

COVER & BOOK DESIGN:
Melanie Gendron

COVER ART:
detail of *THE BEAR DANCE*,
by William Holbrook Beard, ca.1870.
Collection of the New-York Historical Society.

Author Photo by Ted Hall

Library of Congress Number:  2005908253

FIRST EDITION
ISBN: 1-59540-903-3

*for*

**Toby Thompson**

**Leroy Curley**

**Ron Luchau**

**Raqiba Rybicki**

*and in memory of*

**James Welch**

*Mitakuye Oyasin*

# TABLE OF CONTENTS

## PASSAGES

## WALKING, FLYING, STANDING STILL

## GALLERY

## LOST AND FOUND

# WALKING
# BACKWARDS

# POSSIBILITY

First, a cord tightens in your chest
then flame shoots up the back of your neck
your eyes cloud over and your past mistakes
appear like apparitions at a distance.
All you see is what you are and not
what is. Be calm. Draw a bead on them.
Even if you have a clean shot, chances
are they will elude you. If you could only
shake the fever, and quit the fight to
bend them to your will. Kneel here
in the surf. With this thimble, how long
will it take you to empty out the sea?
In truth, your thirst created a mirage.
But look...there is *another* ocean,
inside this one. Toss your thimble out
as far as it will go, and then jump in.

# PASSAGES

# INDIAN SUMMER

But one October evening
you watch me in workclothes
climb up an oak to prune
the raccoon bridge to our eaves
and call out to me to
look at the sky to the west
where a man is followed
by others like him
drunk on the wine of harvest

they begin to sing
the names of things
in voices like webs of
human possibility
past Six-Mile Creek
past the house of black air
past definitions
past the bones
rising to the surface

and down below me
flames dart out of your eyes
and I hug this tree
in a snow of light
the words
frozen to my tongue

4

# RUN, LATE NOVEMBER

I thought it was silence, then the void
materialized, seven of them,
deer, etched and springing, a chorus,

fugue, glissando of deer singing
the white air to life. An antlered
trio cut from the frieze and turned

toward me, turned the white moon up
on the antlers of the grove.
I was running the road through the

graves when the night spilled its eyes
on my spine. Deer, seven, and three
veered to face me, one seasoned in

the moonlight. The sky filled with shapes
I knew—the plainsong of the dead
living with me all these years.

# LOVE SONG

## 1

Five drainages west of here
is the town where you were born;
all the men must register their fists,
the stiff wind makes the women lean,
and outright sanity is treason—
no more than a snoose stain on the map.
But it was you who showed me
inside the mirrors here, the secret
entrance into flowers, to hear
the wind in a different register.

## 2

Thunder from the belly of the sky,
then the sheen of rain on your face.
I kissed you under a wild plum
split by lightning. A willing virgin.
Your blue panties fell to your ankles
and you flicked them with your foot.
I caught them and inhaled your wildness.

## 3

Lips thick and numb from kissing
you come up from the headwaters
where three rivers meet, your bush

halfway between foxred and tawny,
your clothes behind me on the bank.

**4**

You wanted to open your life,
all the parts of you. When that thin song
crawled out from you, I refused
to listen. If I'd known how to let you
you'd have sunk your hand in my heart,
spat in my ears, scratched the rime
from my eyes: healed me. But I
couldn't keep my black beast down.

Soon I was out on the last spit
of existence and I couldn't swim;
you saw a man stepping in
to disaster. When you walked away
that day, your hips receding, I knew
my wings would no longer lift me.
I called out to you, but my words
were pillowed by the fog. Then,
one day, the sun turned black.

**5**

A small hand twisted in your palm
like a pet lizard: your first son.
The loneliness had fallen from you.
You had married well, they told me.

7

Another time, I saw you huddled
like a bat, sifting acorns with a
taped-up rake, then bagging leaves,
a dumb suburban custom. I could
write you off, detach my soul from you.

## 6

At odd times, when snow flicks on the skylight
or a soft wind sucks across a slim piazza,
Charleston, I hear it. When I flail the stretched
catgut with bleeding fingers, your voice,
your voice stampedes up my spine. Your eyes,
the beam of Hatteras circling in the fog,
in low clouds of Prussian blue slinking
over Inverness. In the air where sheep graze
on cold lace near Rannoch Moor, in the breath
of fresh baked bread. In Bombay, I saw
falcons waiting on the rooftops,
you, perched in the scaffolds of my pain.
Oh, God forbid our feeble destinies!

In a dream I was lost.
I canoed through a sinking swamp.
My paddle hit the cartilage heads—
the fish wakened in the coagulum
as the rains came. Druid mudmen,
golem, maybe, hidden in the banks
waited for my will to flag, and then
your gray-blue eyes from somewhere.

**7**

When you entered the room
I pressed my body back in the chair
to keep from taking flight.
Under the fabric, your breasts
turned up at me. Fifteen years
to the day, and your broken words
still wind around my legs and I
cannot walk away. We walk together.

Yesterday we slanted up a draw;
time brings neglect, the land, buck naked.
Your boots brushed against dry pods
of sage lilies, ancient maracas,
and the ground was hollow underfoot.
That inscrutable music, and the set
of your step, told me that you had
weaned yourself from these dry hills.

**8**

My body fell into the light of you
and the swallows brought me back.
A linen blouse on the chair,
a stone jar in the corner. The wind
dissolved your wrists where I kissed them.
One last note of the giant bell reverberates.
The morning took you off as if it owned you.
Your face *was* perfect, now you can't change it.

Your breasts, perfect— the aureoles
not a knob or wen. Why do
two souls refuse what the syllables
spell just beneath cognition?
Blessed is the wall of silence
which rains down behind my lies.
Can I come back to these places,
this same air, beneath your long fingers?

# DOWN RIVER

*for Toby Thompson*

Listen for the scherzo
in the sap of the headwind

listen for the fingerprint
under the tongue

listen for the chairs
of conjuration

listen for tolerance
prudence and blooms

And if it leads you
to several nebraskas

on horseback
with broken exhibits

sit down with me
in the eyehigh stubble

and I'll interpret
I'll interpret

# AS THE DROUGHT BEGINS

the dusks are hard dry knots

   in failing light
    a tiger tom, almost blond
muscles through the yard
      and yowls at the door to be let in
    though he's wild
      and wears a crown of burrs

the dog doesn't even raise his head

     a squadron of fireflies
   cruises the shoals

     a young boy
         comes up from the ravine
and sets down a small shellacked house
     near the garden
    he dusts something on the beans
       in a high rasped chant
     it is not language
it needs to be
    something reptiles understand
     the early bats
       veer down on the sound

outside the town
    other boys, sharp-edged and pale
       emerge from the fields
   and shake the dust
from voices
   their mothers have forgotten

# FIRST POEM

This is the first poem under the sun—
the roaming lateness invites the light
to ride the blessings into evanescence—
a man rhymes water with earth,
a dog climbs the sunrise on the bluff,
a salamander steps slowly from the embers,
a sheep with two heads competes against itself—
light bursts this vessel of my transformation.
Enough listening to the kestrel in the wind,
enough trudging with the turtle in the pasture,
mudmaking enough with the children's children—
I cannot walk alone back there, on the rim,
in the copse, in the grove, in the meadow—
it does not belong to my eye and when I hear
it singing I will not write it down for others—
I can only carry its song in my throat where
it will spill on those I meet,
I can only carry this song
beyond the bluff,
down the valley
to the few families there
and the solitary
who cants his head to hear it,
his odd hat and his troubled shuffle.
I can only sing it
once a lifetime.

# ARBOR NIGHT

At the end of August
        in a summer
    when the heavens
    have disgorged themselves
        ad infinitum
            and the gangly tomatoes
        have just begun to ripen
        the rains
    start up again this evening.

You call me to the back porch
            to witness the presentation:
    the fireflies have all assembled
    in the foliage of the lilac bush
            their lights pulse
        like fading Chinese lanterns
            through the mist.

# OASIS

Where the land tilts down to catchpond
and the air tastes of rusty chain
where fireflies signify over pea-green scum
and the woods itch
impatiently
coyotes weave daybeds
and, intense as phosphorus
set off by campfire moon
shun all at once the possibility of redemption.
You might scent too the Devil's fetid overcoat
hanging in a cottonwood.
Amphibian choruses
ratchet Devonian shape notes
denying the body vanishes.
And what of Lazarus?
Does he remember any of it?
One hundred crows
in the stamen of sleep?
The basilisk doe
and the milkwhite fawn?

# BERRYING GROUND

In pulmonary shade
the blackcaps gape
like a million compound eyes.
Edging through concertina prickers
I can't help myself—
I fondle them
with purple fingers;
blood beads swallow my tongue,
seeds pop my teeth.
There's bear scat everywhere.
Wasps ride my hair
to a tunnel through the canes.
One eye
sees the ebony blastulas,
the other, the golden head
of my son, chirping hosannas
as he pretends to pick,
only half oblivious;
I would swallow fire for him.
Three crows, silent, overhead.
Tonight the moon will be our apricot.

# WHITE SPACE

**1**

I love these days of white space,
empty pages waiting. For anything.
For footprints the wind heals over,
for owls, later, hooting po-po-popopourri

then sweeping up the place. The sloped
shoulders of the barn are solid white.
Even the ponies have long white beards,
even the shadows are empty.

**2**

Full moon through the sunburst locusts,
branches iced and dancing, like zhivago
wind chimes. Just look up and listen.

This is not apocryphal—we saw it
only moments ago. And the apocalypse
wasn't slouched down behind the bluffs.

**3**

From your deer stand, in late November,
before trees silhouette, then disappear,
there's a held breath. A rift between worlds.

What is missing from the rough draft
was not left out—looking is not seeing—
the colophon is out there in the rock.

Some call it atmospheric perspective
sketched in the margins of the mountains
—these notes, more cryptic, with lacunae

where you have to guess. Inhabit the stand
of dead junipers warped in human forms.
Where have you been? What are you being?

One bird. Two notes. Enough to name it.

# LOOMS

## 1

When I spread your placenta on the kitchen counter
your umbilicus was already stiffening. I divided it:
one part each to your two brothers, one to your mother.
I keep mine in a brass canister. Tough as a pumpkin stem.

## 2

Your voice at bedtime is like soft birds falling on the pillows.
At six, you've memorized my scent as I lie next to you and read.
If it were stoppered in a vial, in 50 years you'd recognize me
    instantly.
And where will I be then? And where will you?

## 3

Go out where I can still see you, just as the sun is rising.
The big maples in the front yard answer the horses—listen!
they'll tell you what it's like to have your lungs fill up with bees—
that's one verse. Another: you can sing and fly at the same time.

# NEIGHBORS

The house gone one hundred
thirty years, not a single
speck left of it. Last year
we backfilled the well
so that no small spectator
might fall to gothic gloom.

I can't say I love the tree
but I'd like to, in theory—
to sit under it in bee time
feel the kundalini snap
at a rattler coiled on
the overgrown path
hear the pop when a
buck bites into windfall
come October.
                    Will I
ever prune this veteran
or its consorts? Groom it
otherwise? Bring it three
white stacks of boxes
filled with bee transplants?
These denizens will
outlive me, but maybe
I can ease their passage.

# WALKING, FLYING, STANDING STILL

# WHITTLING THE WIND
*for Boris Gregoric*

Near the end of the gathering
they presented me
with the wing of an angel—
it had been in the family
for generations
brittle but still shimmering.
The angel had fallen
and they'd removed its wings
with a knife—
the other wing
had disappeared.

# CROW PARTS

## 1

eight crows follow
       a great horned owl
    from the ravine
       where I wander
after an ice storm

     three of them land
        to inspect the seeds
           I've cast on the ground
     not to partake
     but to assess—
        bosses, bullies
       condottieri

## 2

three crowshadows
       pass over
    and land
          across the ravine
  watching

they repeat me to each other:
    *human   harmless*
    *eyehunter only*

shredded plastic in the trees
    whiff of tomcat—
        me in my old flannel shirt

## 3

Your mentor, the cut of his beak
    the same as yours, stalls in mid-air
    and freefalls to the ground
        In a minute he'll be up again
    to backtrack north
scouting roadkill, scouting refuse
    making mock
        brash echo
            over the frozen world
And you, underling        the light
    cudgels your black eyes
        as you edge up the branch
    for better vantage
        and drop a load on the rabble
        perched below
      push off your sibling
    through the gray void of the clearing
      Crow talk     *yawk yawk yawk*
      chough bluff
    sharp tongues      black eyes
        open your beak
        open your black eyes
stare inside the beads of corn

in the snow below
You, Crow, from the tribe of trimmers


**4**

31 crows
     in the dendrites of an oak
   silent against the pale moon
      facing southwest


**5**

some human buzz below—
     it looks up, tries to make us
     fly backwards

# HARBINGER

Good Friday, dusk. One coyote comes in close
and circles the house. When I look out at 5 a.m.
he is still there, lurching around the brick corner
tongue out like a pink tortilla. The cats hide
in the stale crawl space. I take out my eyes
and put them on the windowsill, light them
before the sun rises, and the coyote goes away.

# MOVING

the point I wish to make
        or even earlier
    was an interloper
        his scavenged remains
in a cottonwood grove
      we do not know
    the talus to the river
the inner sanctum
      where the wind stopped
    the earth from his bowels
        killed everything
     planted seed    went to sleep
      the stars were strewn
  on the open wound
       and healed it
     open wounds
or dens in the high ridges
     the black speck moving
  was Coyote
      every trick they knew
  he knew better

29

# AT THE TROUGH BEHIND ANDERSON'S, 1957

Used to be a dog I remember
a dog I remember used to be
here at sundown, sundown when
you couldn't see but silhouettes
of the dog and the other critters
dog silhouette, and the others, at sundown

Once a bobcat, sneaking out
from the sunglare, sneaking out to eat
right next to it and it bolted
hackles raised and it ran to the sun
but the cats and possum held their ground

I remember. I forget, sure, sometimes
right, but forget it forever I
never will. It didn't mean
much then and the bobcat and the dog
were gone for good, until today
when I remembered them, the silhouettes.

# THE RED AND BLACK
*late March, northern Wisconsin*

Along Highway 51, where the Bad River
wanders out of earshot, snow pelts my windshield
like huge white diatoms. I make out a roadsign
which says **BEAR HABITAT**. Farther into
this sea of pummeling I sense I must get to the bottom.
Then I hear them calling: "Slow, slow...
turn off into the birches— park your van and leave it...."
I pull my hands up into my sleeves and listen—
"The snow will cover your tracks to our dens—
they cannot follow you. And when it stops you
will have to walk backwards the way you came here.
But how long a song it will be until tomorrow
and what your footprints will resemble is another
story altogether. We are waiting, brother."

# OUTRIDERS

If you think those trees, those birches
out there at the edge of the clearing
are sedentary, then think again—
next year their seedlings will set in
and in five years their saplings
and in twenty they'll fill this space,
and their mavericks will take wing
to wind up over that ravine
that low range that lake and sing
back to these others on the wind.

# SOUTH DAKOTA

East of the river
      they raise one finger
    from the steering wheel in greeting
   West of the river
       they give you the whole hand

# THE BORDER

I have secrets I will tell no one,
not even you, waiting across the border.
I set out over the slackjawed prairie—
every village marked by a white letter
high on the side of a hill with acne,
and all the other signs along the way:
the snake shedding its skin, pale blind eyes;
a dead crow, limp, blood on its pointed tongue;
the juvenile eagle trying to lift the duck
with a broken neck, but it cannot.
Save you, all my friends dead-ended early—
when evening comes, they rise from graves
and a wall of flame, spontaneous,
ignites on the ridge above them.
Though I live alone, every night I return
and there's a crowd around my house.
In my last life I was a good tap dancer
but this time, I've numb clubs for feet.
Nevertheless, one step, then the next.
Between this iris and the river
is a face carved in the shape of my life,
but I'll never see it. I never will.

# GALLERY

# SIBLING

Out in the carport as the sun comes up
my brother is sweet-talking his honey—
a '62 pushbutton Plymouth Fury
that makes the backroads disappear—
Route 161 to Deal Island— gone, vanished.
Route 64 to Snow Hill— kaput.
The windows gulp down swamp air
when he corners like a rat in a barrel.
He told me once "Yeah, you're my brother,
but if you ever lay a hand on me..."
He has his fans, too— the geeks in his class
have parties in his honor when their folks
go out of town. Float beerglasses filled
with Beefeaters out to him in the pool
while he just curls his lip at them and
they just look at each other and say "cool!"
With those gray eyes he could be a sniper;
he could make Julie London sing for more.

# UNBECOMING

Our ex-newspaper carrier
    who looks to be in his early 30's
        and not unschooled
    leaves the Quik-Trip
    with a bottle of Gallo white: 9:45 a.m.
He had delivered the paper sporadically
    and would sling it against the house
with misplaced anger
    I say to the clerk
    "Kind of early in the day for that"
He says "That's his second bottle today. . .
    he stood there at the curb
        and chugged down the first one"
    I fall in behind the man and his bottle
    not even in a bag
Does he recognize me?
He starts fiddling with the seat
    of his unbelted corduroys
    sagging down his ass
    a dark stain already seeping through
where he's shit himself
You can tell it's dribbling down his pantleg
    by the way he wriggles
    He looks around embarrassed
        and our eyes meet just as I

cut across the street
I could have approached him
but I'd recognized the rage in his eyes—
mine of 20 years ago
my rage
buried deeper these days

# ELEGY FOR DARRELL GRAY

We sat around the fire and thought back:
you flew with the last squadron of jackdaws
to circumnavigate the human mind,
and your feeble laugh, commander, was like
self-conscious salt air, your head a home
to 67 varieties of communicable seriocomic self-defeat
not unlike a woodcock drumming in the spring
to the wind from the other northwest place.

When we had remembered all these things
we planted you upright with just your head above ground,
eyes open, facing west with a little
peaked roof on stilts to cover you.
We knew we'd have to sew your mouth shut,
fearing the strange things you'd report back to us.

# SOME BROTHERLY ADVICE

What's the reason your window
stays shut, Bucko? Do you
think you can hang there
on the third floor of the Murray
like a teat on a cow's udder
shrouded in headless emancipation?
You'd reminded me that there were
stipulations which were not
admissible to men on horseback,
that the last time you went into
The Owl at night there was a fat writer
on a toadstool who blew smokerings
out his asshole and he'd called it
"Foursquare Homage to Cabel Hogue."
Consider, now, the Livingston Rodeo,
consider Terpsichore in her tight jeans,
consider Kurt Schwitters and why
he never herded sheep nor line-
danced down at the Old Emigrant Saloon—
you've never had it so good, Junior.
Fill that spot on your head
with sunlight and put distance
in your belly, bro'— Hoyt Axton
ain't axin' you to ride no winged
armadillo to your own redemption—

that's *your* job and you've got
all your teeth left, so
bite in until your jaws go slack.

*Livingston, Montana*

# EBB

Warren, the Potawatomi iron worker
drifted down from the U.P. that spring
and the local sent him up to Johnstown.
He went to work with two fifths of gin
hidden in his toolbox. It was in his
second week when the flood came through and
he took to high ground just as the power blew.
He saw a man get blasted clean through the roof
and land in several pieces on the street.
Warren went to get a closer look. Lost his
breakfast then took a long pull of gin.
A cop came round the corner and took in
the selfsame sight. Warren offered him
the bottle and the two of them just stood there
underneath that sky until they'd drained it.

# THE SHAKING TENT MAN

arrived for ceremonies—
flew in from Canada
waiting for us
at the end of a dock—
We cut saplings for him
set them and pinned the canvas
That afternoon he prayed for us
from his birdface
and his flying heart
He kept telling me
to listen to the wind
in earnest, every day
His name was Giizhik
*cedar* in Anishinabe
And that night in the rain
the tent whomped back and forth
and we heard a menagerie
from within:
chipmunk, bear, lynx,
badger, others
We half-expected
the tent to break loose
and zoom around like a bottle rocket
He spoke
in the old language

and another elder
lay flat on his back
outside the tent
holding one of the poles
interpreting—
ancestors revealed
unearthed
healing
the blood and spirit
After five hours
in the early morning
he emerged serene
as if he'd just stepped
from a shoeshine and manicure—
he was the channel
but not the agent—
the rest of us were beat
Then in the morning
as the sun arose
he flew north

# TWO BLIND MICE

In the cab of the dump truck was a nest
abandoned by the mother: two pink mice.
Steve said "Put them in one of those work gloves
and step on it– no way they can survive."
You brought them home, called the vet for advice,
started feeding them kittens' formula.
You could see the white of the formula
pass into their stomachs, their intestines.
Their large sleek heads, the delicate pink paws
waving like sprigs of sea anemone,
their sharkslung mouths designed for scavenging,
their little teeth nipping at your fingers.
You called the small one Jimi, for Hendrix,
the large one Gulliver. I saw the way
you let them crawl inside your shirt, the way
you held them to feed them with a dropper.
You kept them in a shoebox filled with felt
and shredded paper, a draped lamp for warmth.
Having an office job it fell to me
to cart the shoebox with me to work.
Knowing this made the secretaries cringe;
I'd lift the felt and they'd start in squeaking.
Jimi lasted the week. That next Monday
I stayed home from work. After quitting time
you swung by the house to drop your lunch box

on the way to the pet store to buy a cage;
Gulliver's eyes were due to open soon—
you planned to take him back to school with you.
But his little bellows had ceased to work.
You held him in your palm, you stroked his tiny
potbelly with your thumb. We put each one
in a separate match box, and sprinkled them
with sacred ash from India, a few
silver leaves of sage from Mesa Verde,
then you covered each with a rose petal
before you closed them up. We taped hand-drawn
red hearts on each coffin, along with
"Om Nama Shivaya" in purple ink.
In the smoldering green of the evening
I dug a hole just south of the bird bath.
You placed them in gently, side by side.
I took your hand and we stood a moment.

Even as a child, you were this way—
a kind of ark. You incorporate this slow
swarm of bees in our horsemint blossoms,
that fat worm on the plantain leaves, whose
portholes glow at night, the doe and fawn
who come to the saltlick, the bluejay, the lark,
the chubby sparrows. Bless the ants in the kitchen,
the cockroach, the mosquito, the deerfly, and the tick.
Praise these creatures for this chance to serve them.
Praise death, as we tamp this earth upon their bodies.
Some day we will burn with them in this earth.

# SPACE CADET

My three-year old's an expert on space.
Yesterday he coerced me into buying
a video titled **NASA— 25 YEARS**.
At home, I pop it in for him
just as I read the fine print:

CHALLENGER DISASTER AND INVESTIGATION

but in this rendition
everything is scientific—
    "Dr. Judith Resnick...
    preparing to put on her egress harness
    and enter the orbiter...
    the teacher-observer Christa McAuliffe
    has been handed an apple by the close-out crew..."
and after lift-off:
    "...a minute 15 seconds (A HUGE FLASH)
    velocity 2,900 feet per second, altitude
    9 nautical miles, downrange distance 7 nautical miles
    (then, after a long pause, in measured tones)
    flight controllers here are looking
    very carefully at the situation....
    obviously a major malfunction..."
    (CROSSING CONTRAILS HURTLE TO THE SEA
    LIKE SPENT FIREWORKS)

From the kitchen, I hear my son
parroting the tech talk:
> "...at T minus 2 minutes and 50 seconds
> retraction of the gaseous oxygen vent hood began....
> this flexing increased
> the gap between the tang and the clevis
> at the location of two rubber O rings..."

I recall the tears, back then
of my older son
for Christa McAuliffe, teacher.
When I peek around the corner
my three-year old
is tracing a graph on the t.v. screen
with his index finger:
> "... slight changes in the
> hydrogen tank pressure telemetry data
> confirm the leak 2.2 seconds later at 66.8 seconds..."

My son, oblivious.


Today, as we walk to the mailbox,
he tells me about the asternauts.
I skip a beat
then tell him it's pronounced asTROnauts.
He says no it's not, and we go
back and forth on it.
Later, he tells his mother
"My dad renamed the asternauts."
He points to a newspaper photo

of Yeager, Glenn and the old-timers
and says "these are asternauts..."
then to the new guys, with Glenn
in his most recent incarnation—
"and *these* are asTROnauts."

       But wait... it can't be Yeager, I realize...
       must be Shepard— Yeager
       was too old, too much the hot dog,
       not a company man.

My son tells me he will go to the moon
and his space ship will have a gumball machine
and Emmet will be his co-pilot
and all his friends can come—
"You can come, too!" he beams
All of us in our A-1 Barney-approved
official astronaut outfits.

What the heck, I tell myself
"asternaut" is close enough
for government work...
and that's just the way
Chuck Yeager would pronounce it.

# FINISHING MERRRILL GILFILLAN'S *CHOKECHERRY PLACES* AT THE CAMBODIAN BUDDHIST TEMPLE, NORTH BRONX

From my window, concrete ziggurat to the southeast,
walls of saffron and orange behind me, incense up the stairs,
calligraphy on posters, a happy embroidery.
I close the book, bundle against mid-March wind and
take to the streets, rambling, past secretive stream
under flyway distorted from below, klakkle of the El,
whoop and slap of milkcrate basketball, to small
Middle Eastern kitchen where I order spicy goat.
Boozy whitemen, of no known ancestry, come and go,
asking for caw-fee and cigarettes, see basmati rice
in heating tray and ask if it is Rice-a-Roni.
I think, on the other hand, of you, my friend
passing through the land, brushing away your footprints
as you go. Your words will not bring misguided pilgrims
to Cherry Creek, the Grand, the Mandan villages—
only others, like yourself, who leave no trace.

# FOR MY KHMER BROTHERS AND SISTERS

*in memory of Haing S. Ngor*

## I

Your eyes offended you so you've plucked them out,
and your left hand has severed the right. You have
sold your skin to make bullboats for crossing the Mekong
but the skin was stretched taut and burst,
drowning your children. You have snapped off the
supple fingers of apsara dancers like stringbeans.
You have pestled the towers of Angkor Wat into dust
and fashioned a highway from Vietnam to Thailand
paved with skulls. You take the red wine of the
blood of your parents and the red meat of your siblings
to fortify your own. You have eaten the raw livers
of virgins you've bludgeoned and your eyes glow
yellow as saffron. You have cut down the vines to eat
and they've risen to life and strangled you.
Your smiles, like a chandelier in a well and your voices,
rivulets over dry red rock. Do you wonder why
all the frogs and dragonflies have disappeared
and the small deer which sing at night and the
geckos and eagles have fled across the borders?
The amethysts turn wet and cowardly and the
fields of sapphires grow gray and thin.
The authorities have arrived from the east
to examine your dreams, and when you look in the mirror,

over your shoulder, there they are, the authorities.
Dams burst and prophecies come true—how long,
how long until the wheel will churn no more?

## II

Blessed are the pure in heart, for they shall wear rags.
Blessed are the blind for they won't see it coming.
Blessed are the lame, for they shall be
thrown from high places, then buried alive.
Blessed are the mothers, as they fall asleep
while their fires die and their wombs fill with dust.
Blessed are the poets, for their tongues shall be
extricated and their words used as tinder.
Blessed are the lovers of beauty, for they
shall bathe in their children's excrement.

# BOMBAY, ESPLANADE
*June 1979*

I skim along green and saffron streets
bathed by monsoon rain. Arabs in white
stroll past in pairs, here for the ablutions.
At the corner, a man on goat cart
sitting on useless legs, extends his hand.
His hand is just a palm, fingers gone.
I place coins on his flesh and travel
down the warrens of his sweet black eyes.
His eyes cut past me to five ravens
raucous in the branches overhead.

# DIASPORA

Our worst case cousins were sent down under
to an island where silence had become.

They had rust for breakfast, head lice for lunch,
coaxed allegories from their cleft songbirds.

Their rooves leaked only on St. Brigid's Day;
otherwise, they lived dry as basilisks.

The old ones dressed for the Apocalypse,
while the young wore fishes in their armpits.

Their keepers had loose lips, parted their hair
stage left, as if awaiting a cotillion.

The simplest margin here was rarely blessed—
diddled if they did, damned if they didn't.

When they died, their souls were sold as roses
to insulate the parlors of the rich.

# FROM WHERE THE SUN NOW STANDS

Head east from Dunkirk, through
Inverness and Kremlin. This side of Zurich,
you reach Chinook. Cut south toward
the Bear's Paw. In a draw on Snake Creek
there are names you can't pronounce:
Ollokot, Heinmot Tooyalaket, Toohoolhoolzote
still thick in the air of late June.

On the first hill, a nesting prairie hawk
flies directly at your head. Yield.
The creek is a seep full of wild roses.
Yellow prickly pear and sage dot the hills—
marrow has nurtured the roses.
It is peaceful here though clouds drop down
like scraps of buffalo robe. Taste
the salt of words and Joseph's broken heart.
Climb to the metal stakes which mark
where they fell, Looking Glass and the others.
No sun. The cloy of gunpowder on your tongue.
The smell of men dug in and and fear,
their precious Apaloosas scattered.
The children starved and freezing.
Some disappeared into the hills.
You kneel in sage stubs, and your tears
salt the ground. The prairie hawk
finally drives you out.

Just north, along a fence line, haystacks.
Nearby, a cat sits opposite three pheasants.
As you approach, the cat slinks away
and the pheasants follow, single file.
They disappear between the bales.
Later, down the Powder River Road
you see a deer and coyote nose to nose.
What they mean is beyond your understanding;
perhaps the kin of those who ran away.
They say this land can break your heart.

*Bear Paw Battlefield, Montana*

# MOOT SUN

Audubon saw it:
a flock, he said, that went on
for two hundred forty miles.

Where they came down, trees
collapsed. On Sundays
men went out with shotguns—

thousands blasted of an afternoon.
The last one shriveled
in the Cincinnati Zoo,

1914. Not one
shows up at the feeder.
Not one in the pines at dusk

as you walk, a different
hooing than you're used to.
Not one. Can the cod

teeming the Grand Banks
vanish? The newt
sidestepping your bootsole

go back into itself? All those
husks of mayflies
bulldozed off the levee

into dust, and the cycle stop?
Will the sun set in the
ocean to the west? Will we

discover we are dogs
kicking our feet in dreams?
Can we ever be happy at this?

Oh, taste of clover
on your tongue. The last
sound before you fall asleep.

The sea of wings
beating down upon the trees.
Swimming under the great
shadows passing overhead.

# LOST AND FOUND

# BITUMINOUS

*St. John's, Newfoundland, 1954*

An unwilling evening, my mother
stood here, filled in with light.

Kittens hung on the screen door
as she baked codfish cakes.

Prevailing westerlies carried
the scent off-shore. In front of

The Basilica, old men
expectorated blue cobblestones.

Our garden grew nothing
but tiny American flags.

# HOW I GOT MY SUMMER VACCINATION

In the summer of my sixteenth year I lived in my overcoat half the day studying geometry and tectonic deuteronomy and blonde girls with high heels and asses. I took classes in typing blood and other body fluids and played baseball in a baseball suit the rest of the time I wasn't holding up the centerpole of the universe. And one time when the nighthawks wouldn't let me sleep and lifting the weight of the world wasn't enough, I took a job at a circus. The circuses came and went and I set them up and tore them down. Carousel parts, chinese red and thickly greased, gears for engines of torture from Bunyan's nightmares. Mildewed canvases, men with cigars, everything smelling of piss, despair and resignation. Objects constantly impaled my palms— filaments of giant bulbs, nails, blades of light spinning out of septic darkness. And the women waited in every shadow, painted designs on my chest and pressed against me. And the fat woman emerged from her trailer every night the same to feed her chihuahua whose front legs had been sawed off and she'd offer it some raw tidbit and its eyes would bug and it would tilt toward the plastic dish until she'd yank the dish away and the little wretch would topple forward on its face and kick its back legs like a frog and a round phlegmish laugh would roll out from her and she'd roll her eyes, thrust her hidden crotch at me, spewing red beans and rice. But in all those blackstrap nights my eyes never once left her face.

*Suitland, Maryland 1959*

# RELEASE ME

and a woman in a red scarf
idles at the curb for me

we comb the back roads
and the old farms we recognize

there are decades of sunlight
sewn into our eyes.

That woman is someone I in-
herit. When we stop to eat

waves on the jetty
cover our advances— we can't

be seen in public. Her song
on everything I remember

her song on everything.

# UNFINISHED BUSINESS

There was the first time we made love—
it was in the shower, a perfect fit
standing up, hand in a fine glove—
more lubricous, of course. Through the slit
of the bathroom window the Bridgers loomed
like a blue wall of ancient thunderheads.
From the start, something about it felt doomed—
you loved me in cars, bars and flower beds;
surrender, a hand I refused to play.
As I turned from you, you climbed a ladder
of hysteria. Three times locked away
and five marriages later, our patter
on the phone is easy as if no time
has passed....

# IN THE TALL HOUSE

In the tall house lined with
beads and begonias in the

blue hills sifted with doves
you offered me your love again

like you offered me the bluefish
you'd caught that afternoon

done up with homegrown
peppers onions and tomatoes

like you offered me a beer.
Your love— "Take it," you said,

again, after all these years
and your gypsy son brooding

in his workshop with his cats
saying later, "Will he stay the

night, which room will he
sleep in, will he be staying?"

# ATLAS AXIS

*the New Atlas Bar,*
*Columbus, Montana*

In the days before
interstate cappuccino
and llama ranch incursion
you'd stop here
before winding up
into westering hills
through a scrim of early snow.
It was your own
delerium tremens in waltz time.
Your conversation
was not so much
with the two-headed patrons
or the barkeep waxing at the tap
but with yourself
as you sat in buffalo coat
your cornucopia
of melancholy on the bar.
If you were sanguine
you'd last the night
and the old-timers
would put you on the clock—
if they suspected
a hidden agenda
you'd disappear into thinner air.

Times have changed now
but not the register –
the New Atlas
holding up the hills
on droll mahogany shoulders.

# SHADES

One  May dusk
in the waning hours of my youth
I left the Pony Bar
and leaned against the wall to smoke
though I didn't
There, some forty miles beyond
stood the Bridgers
in cowboy pastel
Charley Russell colors
Late that August
north and east of there
I saw that backdrop everywhere
And due north
I awoke in Glacier Park
in the late
Tang Dynasty
and laughed
until I wept
It was the summer
this bar became the outpost
I looked back from
always
a golden silt
at the bottom of my beer

One night, I made it with a cowgirl
in a backyard strafed by meteors
another night, a comet
arced the ruins of the hot springs
another, sun storms
opalesced the empty streets
I saw a boy in a gaslit window
with the head of a red-tailed hawk
The barkeep
kept an alternate world
padlocked in the storeroom
She let me see it once
and when I left that night
my heart
split
and its contents
spilled across the big sky

# THE MYOPIC TRAVELLER TAKES A SHORTCUT SOUTH DAKOTA, AUGUST

I cut west on Route 18,
a red road on the map
and in truth the road is—
a pale brick cast, crushed granite,
salt of the earth. The wind
crawls across the farmsteads
to Idlewylde where the sign says
St. Boniface— not bonny,
this one, but boney-face,
to whom they owe obeisance,
who cast his own ashes in the sea.

Shorn lambs in their tatty hides,
barrows and gilts among the
checkerboard Norman silos—
no rhyme here, no reason why
the settlers stayed. Another sign:
Alcester Fair. Sponsored by
the Union County Virgins.
I pull over, piss at a redwing
perched on a post—the ground hisses.
Lightning scours the corn. The cross
wind keeps the wolf from the doors.

Past Davis, I cross the Vermillion—
you can take it north near the shell
of Pumpkin Center. At Olivet,
the Jim, which starts up in a
vinegar plain west of Jamestown.
Just after I've angled north
I gas up at the next hometown.
Their claim to fame's a water tank
shaped like a turquoise teapot.
I take a stool and study
their dialect of silence;
rum and coke's the swill of choice.
Outside the tavern window
I can see the fields on empty.

# IF YOU GO DOWN IN THE WOODS TODAY

I slip from the double sleeping bag
      where we are sacked out illegally
   inside Glacier Park
     walk naked to the nearby creek
  below the falls
    where I begin to wash my penis
      with a bar of soap
      from a night of freighttrain lovemaking
       when I look up and see
           a guide and thirty tourists
      looking down from a hanging bridge
    taking in the wildlife

# WAXWINGS IN EARLY MAY
*for Dr. Hsi Cheng*

We are out at dusk clearing the last of the winter debris from the back yard, watching for the goldfinch we'd seen at the feeder, when a discreet flock of cedar waxwings settles on the neighbor's apple tree among festoons of white, pink and fuchsia. Through the binoculars, we see that they are plucking stamens from the blossoms, sometimes gobbling petal after petal. Now and then one strops its beak clean of ambrosia. And drifts off as if in reverie. Sometimes as few as three of them, as many as ten. This is nothing like their fall behavior when they migrate south—dipping communally in our birdbath, scouring the juniper of fermented berries, crashing into bedroom windows. The sun is about to set and the clear light shooting horizontally across the robin's egg sky hits them so the tawny colors of their breasts are much yellower than their earthen fall plumage, each bird outlined by a thin golden aura. One preens its breast feathers displaying the black undercoat. Another rudders on a branch showing the bright yellow band on its tail. Impeccable dressers, with identical Chinese-red slashes on their wingtips. If I had been an aging master during the Sung dynasty, I would have thrown away all my other paintings and kept this as my single masterpiece.

# ONE SEASON

the dear old pear tree, as Giacometti
had conceived it, spindly,
behind the magnolia and the house
and the little apple
the rabbits crop
and the big apple in the neighbor's yard
where the northward waxwings
stop to dip their beaks
in blossoms
and the deer in later months
collect the windfall
and the grapes on the vine
fermenting
and the mulberry droppings in the grass
the fuschia ruffles of the lilac
guarding the southwest passage
where the stray tom rests
and the elder statesman redbud
ambling horizontal
all within the shadow of the giant oak
where crows sway and
nuthatches skritter down the bark
the bangles on the Solomon's seal
the tea roses white
against the white aslant garage
under which the tame groundhog abides

and grazes down the vetch
the bunnies' nest in the garden enclosed
the cardinals' nest
in the gnarly pines
the black stump where the mushrooms grow
the ghosts of raspberries I uprooted
the fireflies the bats
the cool birdbath
which breathes above the cistern
the other birdbath
where cats imbibe the sky
the mock orange and the hidden plum
the busy chickadees and juncoes
tulips, crocuses and the blowing peonies
poison ivy
and my old heart
in a shallow grave

# SUNDAY NAP

I fall asleep at noon and forget it
is the last day of our relationship—
that I must begin walking backwards
through all my lies and leave you here.

# FROM DOWN THE ROAD

It happens that we leave town the same day.
Her house is newly painted inside and out,
an understated wedgewood—crisp, clean,
pristine, just like her mind. Then there's my
rented room at the back of a place on the edge,
overlooking my garden, which has not gone to
seed but to tangles and huge tumerous tomatoes,
zucchini and eggplants. This is the way they
will remember us. And explain what happened.

# THE CASE OF THE KNUCKLE-HEADED WREN

I have taken the pills which are supposed to
make me sleep but cause my penis to swell up
and sway like a turgid viper every morning at 5 a.m.

And at 5:15, the wren, that little pedant, comes to
sing his one-verse mating song over and over
outside my window on the bluebird house he's

filled with sticks. I slam the door, I close all four
windows, turn on the fan— nothing helps.
I get up and move the bluebird house down

to the garden, hang it at the middle of the bean
fence, where it looks like a church poor box.
Immediate traffic, as other wrens begin to case it.

An hour later, my wren is back, perched in the
branches of the dead pussy willow, singing his same
droll melody. What kind of mate would that attract?

Some left-brained Skinnerian moron. I get up again
and tell him off, explain my situation to him,
that I haven't had a good night's sleep in six months.

He gives me respite, but an hour later is right back
at it. I get up, have a decent breakfast, bowel movement,
get dressed, then take down the pruning shears and

lop the pussy willow free of branches. With my ax,
hack the rest to a central stump with amputated aorta,
arteries, etc. At noon the wren shows up again,

at cat level on the stump. He sings away, with a few
missed notes this time, trying to figure what has happened,
how he can sell anyone on this as a decent proposition.

# CONSTITUTIONAL

a ten-mile walk
        in 100° heat
    along highway shoulders
cans flattened to rusty skimmers
            snakes pressed to parchment
    I pocket endless
dead butterflies and cabbage moths
            as I pull for home

    three blocks from where I live
    a pair of cecropia moths
mate calmly on an uncut lawn
            like bonsai Japanese kites
        or tattooed manta rays
            barely pulsing in the shallows
    I stretch out next to them
            then the male lifts off
to the green gloom
            across the street
    while the female's
    red striated abdomen
            convulses several times

    I'd be content to fall right here
        and have my bones reduced to dust

# BOB'S SWEAT

It rained straight through that August.
In my windowless office, it didn't.
Old flames burned through the damp
and I headed north because I did.
I got one lake short of the border.
It was raining there, everywhere.
Vines had braided the frame of Bob's lodge.
Root beer kept exploding in the crik.
I slept up in the Norwegian shed.
Bob worked a burn in that rain
and came home every day to
Inez and kids black as a coal miner.
It rained. I walked the rivers
and the downfall, thinking of my own.
And one night, in the rain, he
popped up his bright blue poly
ice fishing shack with the hole
in the floor, shovelled hot rocks in
and said let's get to it. By then,
the wind was woofing and the
lodgepoles lashed each other.
We sang over the din, old songs.
Then whap! three lodgepoles
fell on the sagging roof and
he said "Now we're *really* cookin!"

Hoppy, the three-legged Husky
scratching to get in— we let him
poke his nose through the flap
but he only sneezed at the sage
and backed away. Har-de-har-har!
Orion, animated as a doodle bug,
shimmied bare-ass through the flap
with teeth clacking from the cold.
Out for a breather in the gale.
Clear the nostrils, shiver back in.
Again. Again. Again. What it meant,
what it means, both silent and aloud,
can't be drowned or burned or
walked away from. One night,
in the rain, a drum from somewhere.

# REINS

After twenty years, you travel north to see me,
with your teenage daughter as a chaperone;
the gray in our hair becomes the both of us.

You had a taste for sailing close to shore
where the lilies of eccentricity slowed you;
that's where you found me, in select company.

I remember long indigo afternoons,
words of smoke, stars imbedded in my skin,
stolen lifetimes in Charleston and Manhattan.

Though I knew you'd never give up everything
I waited, but didn't have the grit to ask;
my outlook sank like a weighted corpse.

I moved. Our letters sleepwalked back and forth.
When your first child was born, I was silent
for two years, because he wasn't mine.

We sit here, silent. Beyond the porch, horses
loll in purple loosestrife. Your daughter and
my five-year old son wonder, palpably.

The woman I love now, stands at the door
with tea, and knows I will not turn away
though once I would have done most anything.

82

# JOURNAL 27 AUGUST 2000

Maples sprout in grasses
fringing the half-built house.
The two pups chase phantoms
in long Sunday shadows.
Through a cleft in the bluffs
the river turns at 90 degrees.
The smell of workmens' urine
mixed with goldenrod.
Gothic buckthorns line the fence.
200 years ago, the bluffs were bare,
now menageries of trees;
I count 23 species as I walk.
Steady chirr of crickets: the undertone
of powerlines. Queen Anne's lace
folds in on itself: settings for fantastic gems.
Solo dragonfly going home to base.
Three turkeys flush up into the oaks—
both dogs run straight past me
ears flying, all the way home.
From backside of the berry patch
a buck snorts his warning.
I pick ten plump ones—last of the season.
Two ridges over, reports from the gunclub—
planks dropped against each other.

As I enter the woods, a weight
drags the center of my chest.
I stand, breathing, keeping it at bay
until it passes. Several times a week now,
no warning and no reason.
If I wait too long, this could
be the last fall I walk this path,
inhale Queen Anne, taste
blackberries on my tongue,
the river in blue distance.

Since I was fifteen I've courted her—
led her on, been fickle: if you betray me
I'll betray you back. Her toes
were licorice, her breath like
currants in a rusty pipe, her flesh,
the Rubicon, the Danube and the Nile—
the deepest summer of my life
but it never ended. If you add it
all together, maybe one month
out of my entire life. I always
went home with Grushenka.
But this time she means
to have her way with me.

I write a few words a day
with a thick carpenter's pencil,
enough to keep the yellowjackets
spinning, to fill the emptiness
between her visits.

# PROCEDURE
*for Orion*


After the Three Wild Babylonian Baboons
walk off in the rain, eating bread and butter
and we snuggle, you drop off into deep sleep.
I uncradle your head from my right arm,
and kiss you one more time. Hibernating
you clutch your spellbound sequined iguana....

Nothing unusual on the farm tonight—
a yearling nickers in the dark corral,
soft blue snowlight slats through the blinds
and makes the plastic stars on the wall
glow in the shape of your constellation.
The radiators code talk in response.

                    ....Tomorrow morning
I must rise early and go to the place where
they will snake the passages to my heart
and determine the damage I have done.

I must return from this to you. I must.
To watch you rise, and be my sun again,
to live life closer to the earth and sky,
to sing the stillness at the root of things.

# ALL AROUND THE CIRCLE
*St. John's, Newfoundland, 1949-1955*


Cousin Jack perched on Temperance Street
    which, if you weren't (temperate), and stumbled
you'd tumble to an oily harbor grave. Their house
    on a slant and their back garden
space for five or six to sit and sing or speculate.
    Their doors were painted the colors of the circus.
Jack drove a Morris Minor
    parked somewhere flat above their alley.
Seagulls skreeled in heavy air of the codfish catch.
    Jack was a terrier,
with the crinkly eyes of all my mother's kin.
    His dory stashed in a grotto of the harbor.
In spring, he'd putt-putt us out the Narrows
    to look down icebergs—their ghost cetacean bodies
sighed and seethed over onto their backs. Took us fishing
    inland, up pine-needled mooseroads where
every flycast brought a leaping running rainbow
    I was too afraid to knock unconscious. The
smell of trout, his pipe, coffee in his thermos
    and Sunday news on the radio from Antigonish
or crazy reels from baymen run amuck in Ottawa.


    In those days, coal incensed the air and quirky sailors
took their smokes from Players' cavalier square boxes.
    We'd wait 'til they'd toss their butts then gather 'em

in our Walter Raleigh tins for later beneath the steps
        of the movie house— where Olivier moped in shadow
and Ophelia sang as she floated down the stream.
        Fortified with day-old crullers
we wee curmudgeons congregated there to swap
        our views of Miss Lilly's cantilevered Maidenform
or what it was like to be Christine Jorgenson, or to
        feel up a sunglassed Princess Margaret on the Riviera.
A dime would get you in the picture show, and a dime would buy
        a G.I. Joe or Straight Arrow or Green Hornet.
G.I. Joe, a minor league pitcher from East Turncoat, Tennessee
        who could ricochet a grenade off three trees, three cave
        walls and into
a Korean machine gun emplacement...but beware!—
        in the next month's issue, the "Yellow Peril" swept over
        the hill
in unending waves of gray padded coats, two-toed shoes
        and threatening dentition.
In the light, I inhaled road appled sunny macadam,
        girls with rosy-cheeks and button eyes
who flashed white cotton panties jumping rope
        who breakfasted on white bread and molasses
'til their teeth turned black by the age of twelve.
        In my pocket, ha'pennies polished smooth
each one worth five sticks of licorice.


        I remember passing boys on the road
one fateful day, holding up their string of trout
        for us to appreciate, and my mother stopped the Nash

to chat. Their smiles and muscled trout
        ignited the afternoon. But the next day,
a grainy photo of one of them, Ignatius Crotty,
        struck by a hit-and-run and rendered
in the words of our babysitter Alma,
        Salvation Army Major, "simple."


I feared the orphanage we played in basketball
        because it was Catholic and I was not.
As I left the coal-heated gym
        on my way to take a leak down darkwood tunnels
I thought a priest would kidnap me,
        brainwash me into "The Faith"—
the years would reveal my instincts had some basis.


        And once a year, Portuguese in parti-colored shirts
swam swarthy arm-in-arm down Water St.,
        watering the cobbles with their ample manhoods.
Our world was simple then, a heartbeat
        which, once a week, in the woods, revealed
a lichened horse's skull we thought a dinosaur.
        Always the echoes of a horse-drawn hearse
clomping from The Basilica.
        It was a time before spandex, before Prozac, before indoor
        baseball
when every potato mound
        was fertilized with codfish heads.

As the one American in my school
    I responded to the taunts, then
slunk my wounds through coal-dust streets,
    with ripped patch on my school blazer,
to be spanked at home for fighting.
    In spring, there were walking races—
attenuated men, Flemish Jesuses,
    angling in from the outports
white handkerchiefs knotted at the corners
    to keep the pale sun from their tonsures.
Two worlds, two parks: Bannerman, sedate, Victorian;
    Bowring, where families picnicked
and every man with a fag on his lip
    and a chip on his pint-sized shoulder.

Up hills where forts were hidden
    in heat of summer, were mongrels digging rats
midst prickers holding tart pale globes of gooseberries
    rabbits napped in rafts of elfhedge
ornamented with exploding blueberries
    the faint taste of faerie dust on currant bushes
and then the miniature succulent sacred hearts of strawberries.

    In autumn, pencil cases, tepid milk in thermoses
and fields of solid mud behind board fences
    where young boys booted up against each other.
Ships hooted lonely in the harbor.
    The R.C.M.P., red-coated colossuses

89

stood and saluted us on the way to our painting classes.
  From sources unbeknownst
a bottle of cod liver oil for every snot-nosed angel.
  And sprinkled with vinegar, fish and chips
on yesterday's news, seasoned the evening.


  In winter, snow concealed the telephone poles
and we made labyrinths
  collapsed by dogs and younger brothers.
Sleigh races on the ice of Quidi Vidi
  and tales of when the ice gave way.
In the stores, there were seal paper weights, seal
  cutlets, coats and tea cosies
which no one in that third world could afford.
  But everyone owned Coronation teacups.


In coves, tumescent eels would graze your legs,
  and once a year, capelin swarmed your ankles.
In every barren, albino moose
  yellow as nicotine.
The smell of trout and woodsmoke
  permeated tweed
and caribou velvet
  was graphite on your fingers.
I watched and listened, tasted everything,
  in the Land Where Potholes Were Invented.
Three times, from Signal Hill, I saw the Spirit
  move from sea above to sea below.

And when we left, fog held us back a week—
      finally airborne, to the States of my adolescence.
I was never meant to be a gentleman—
      a bayman forever, by choice, by predilection.
The names keep calling me: Garnish,
      Come-by-Chance, Bay L'Argent
Gaff Topsail, Fogo, the Exploits River
      Witless Bay, Virgin Arm
Leading Tickles, Pouch Cove, Heart's Content....

*for my brothers John and Jim*
*and in memory of Jack and Ted Withers*

# ABOUT THE AUTHOR

Ken McCullough's most recent books are *Obsidian Point* (2003) and *Left Hand* (2004). He has received numerous awards for his poetry including the Academy of American Poets Award, a National Endowment for the Arts Fellowship, a Pablo Neruda Award, a Galway Kinnell Poetry Prize, the New Millennium Poetry Award and the Capricorn Book Award. Most recently, he received grants from the Witter Bynner Foundation for Poetry, the Iowa Arts Council, and the Jerome Foundation to continue translating the work of U Sam Oeur. *Sacred Vows,* a bilingual edition of U's poetry with McCullough's translations, was published in 1998. U's memoir (written with McCullough), *Crossing Three Wildernesses*, was published in 2005. McCullough was born in Staten Island, N.Y. but spent his formative years in St. John's, Newfoundland and regards the mountains of Montana and Wyoming as his spiritual home. He has been adopted into the Miniconjou band of the Lakota Nation. After a fairly nomadic life, McCullough has settled in Winona, Minnesota with his wife Lynn and son Orion. His older son Galway is an actor in New York.

# ACKNOWLEDGEMENTS

"The Myopic Traveller Takes a Shortcut, South Dakota, August," "Release Me" and "Two Blind Mice" appeared in *Rain City Review*; "Moving," "South Dakota" and "If You Go Down in the Woods Today" appeared in *A Longhouse Reader*; "If You Go Down in the Woods Today" was reprinted as a postcard by *Red Dragonfly Press*; "Unfinished Business" appeared as "Semiotics" in *Libido* and was reprinted in *Firestarter*; "Crow Parts" appeared in *Confluence*; "Some Brotherly Advice" appeared in *Black Buzzard Review*; "Indian Summer" appeared in *Old Crow*; "Bob's Sweat" appeared in *Briar Cliff Review*; "Elegy For Darrell Gray" appeared in *Abraxas*; "For My Khmer Brothers and Sisters," appeared in *Abiko Quarterly* (Japan); and was anthologized in *From Blue Herons to White Cranes*; "The Case of the Knuckle-Headed Wren" and "At the Trough Behind Anderson's, 1957" appeared in *More Than Animals* (anthology), Redtail Books; "From Down the Road" and "Arbor Night" appeared in *100 Words*; "Run, Late November," and "Love Song" appeared in *Nimrod*; "Atlas Axis" appeared in *Big Sky Journal*; "Ebb" appeared in *Steam Ticket, a Third Coast Review*; "Whittling the Wind," "The Red and the Black," and "Down River" appeared in *The Iowa Source;* "The Red and Black" was anthologized in *Grrrr- A Collection of Poems About Bears*, Arctos Books; "Unbecoming" and "Constitutional" appeared in *Slipstream;* "In the Tall House" appeared in *Dominion Review;* "Sibling" appeared in *Pleiades;* "Outriders" and "How I Got My Summer Vaccination" appeared in *North Coast Review;* "Waxwings in Early May" appeared in *South Dakota Review;* "Small Revelation at the Sundance" and "Bituminous" appeared in *Mosaic;* "Shades" appeared in *Montana Crossroads Magazine;* "One Season" appeared in *Great River Review;* "Reins" and "Journal 27 August 2000" appeared in *River King Poetry Supplement;* "Finishing Merrill Gilfillan's Chokecherry Places at the Cambodian Buddhist Temple, North Bronx" appeared in the *2001 Minnesota Poetry Calendar*, Black Hat Press, and was anthologized in *33 Minnesota Poets,* Nodin Press; "Possibility," "As the Drought Begins," and "The Shaking Tent Man" appeared in *No Exit;* "Procedure" and "White Space" appeared in *Luna;* and "White Space" was anthologized in *From Blue Herons to White Cranes;* "From Where The Sun Now Stands" appeared in *The Evansville Review;* and was anthologized in *From Blue Herons to White Cranes;* "Diaspora" and "First Poem" appeared in *The North Stone Review;* "The Border" appeared in *Water-Stone;* "Neighbors" appeared in *The Mochila Review;* "Moot Sun," "Oasis" and "Harbinger" appeared in *Gingko Tree Review;* "All Around The Circle" appeared in *New Millennium Writings* and was the winner of the New Millennium Poetry Award for the year 2000, and "Elegy for Darrell Gray," "Outriders," and "The Red and Black" were reprinted in *Walking Backwards*, a Longhouse Publishers chapbook. "Waxwings in Early May" and "How I Got My Summer Vaccination" were included in *Left Hand*, Seismicity Editions.

**Special thanks to the Ucross Foundation, The Iowa Arts Council and The Jerome Foundation.**

OTHER BOOKS BY KEN McCULLOUGH

# POETRY

*The Easy Wreckage* (1971)

*Migrations* (Chapbook, 1972)

*Creosote* (1976)

*Elegy for Old Anna* (1985)

*Travelling Light* (1987)

*Sycamore.Oriole* (1991)

*Obsidian Point: A Tripych* (2003)

*Walking Backwards* (Chapbook, 2003)

# TRANSLATIONS

*Sacred Vows* (translations from Khmer
of poems by Cambodian poet U Sam Oeur, 1998)

# PROSE

*Left Hand* (2004)
*Crossing Three Wildernesses*
(memoir by U Sam Oeur
co-written with Ken McCullough, 2005)

Printed in the United States

Printed in the United States
41356LVS00002B/1-39